SEVEN DEADLY SINS

THE UNCOMFORTABLE TRUTH

DAN BOONE

BEACON HILL PRESS
OF KANSAS CITY

Library of Congress Cataloging-in-Publication Data

Boone, Dan, 1952-
Seven deadly sins : the uncomfortable truth / Dan Boone.
    p. cm.
    ISBN 978-0-8341-2360-1 (pbk.)
 1. Deadly sins. I. Title.

BV4626.B66 2008
241'.3—dc22

2007048184

10 9 8 7 6 5 4 3 2 1

CONTENTS

ACKNOWLEDGMENTS

The sense of right and wrong comes very early in life. It is to be credited to the activity of the Holy Spirit, mediated through the influence of the people of God. My primary early mediators were my parents, Algie and Ruth Boone. Dad worked for Sears Roebuck and earned the trust of a town in his business dealings. His ethics were compassionate, honest, and without guile. Mom stayed home and raised three children in the most loving and disciplined atmosphere imaginable. If I could clone my childhood home, it might save the world.

Obedience to God and avoidance of sin, especially the deadly ones, can be achieved by two ways. Either you are so afraid of getting caught with your hand in the cookie jar, and the consequences that would follow; or love was so pure that you could not bring yourself to offend it. I was shaped by both. The first, early in life; the last, later. And now love compels me.

There are many people in the balcony of my life, before whom I live each day. But I will forever be grateful to my parents for their early influences and gracious sacrifice.

Thanks, Mom and Dad,
Dan

AUTHOR'S NOTE

Some excuse their sin by the statement, "I'm only human." To be accurate, God created humanity without and prior to sin. In the garden story, sin arrives late on the stage of history. It might be better said that sin—the deadly sins in particular—signifies that we are not "fully human." For this reason it is fitting that the seven deadly sins are often associated with animals, one animal for each sin.

The bear symbolizes anger.
Envy is represented by the dog.
The pig, fittingly, represents gluttony.
Sloth is represented by the goat.
The horse symbolizes pride.
Lust is represented by the cow.
Greed is represented by the frog.

The positive side to this uncomfortable truth is that each sin is also paired with a heavenly virtue, demonstrated most clearly in the life of Jesus.

For anger, forgiveness.
For envy, kindness.
For gluttony, temperance.
For sloth, diligence.
For pride, humility.

AUTHOR'S NOTE

For lust, chastity.
For greed, charity.

May we be delivered from our subhuman likeness to animals, and be fully restored to our humanity which is defined as holiness, sanctity, or Christlikeness.

INTRODUCTION: THE "S" WORD

A generation ago, the word *sex* was a whispered word. Rarely was it said out loud in public. Some even referred to it as "the *S* word." But not anymore. It's on TV, radio, billboards, book titles, coffee mugs, talk shows, T-shirts, magazine covers, car ads, and half-time shows. Sex is no longer the taboo topic. "The *S* word" has lost its rare-sighting status, and another word has taken its place.

Sin.

Saying *sin* in public is like saying *bomb* on an airplane. People get uncomfortable and intense scrutiny is likely to follow.

So we don't say *sin.* We say foul-up, goof, blunder, wrong, mistake, foible, infraction, error in judgment, flaw, addiction, weakness, shortcoming—but we don't say sin. And this wouldn't be so bad if sin itself had disappeared like other seldom-said words—like bubonic plague, or turntable.

Has sin disappeared? Is it possible that while we slept last night, the last vestige of sin slowly crept off the planet and left us in the uncontaminated state of Eden?

January 2007. I checked the Saturday morning paper in
Nashville.

A federal judge is under investigation.

People are shooting deer in developing
subdivisions, making mothers fearful for their
children.

Lawsuits abound, suggesting that "somebody
done somebody wrong."

Gulf Coast insurance companies are
cheating their policy holders out of
Katrina benefits.

Ozone levels are rising from increased auto emissions.

A coach and a general manager are saying unkind
things about each other.

The Tennessee Lottery is bilking the poor to
finance education in the state.

A body is found at Percy Priest Lake.

Update on Iraq: another suicide bomber.

Some of the movies are risqué.

Embryos are for sale in Texas, complete with a
list of donor characteristics.

Abortion rights folk are excited about
new leaders in Congress.

A letter to the editor complains about racism.

The minimum wage—yes or no, and is it a moral
issue?

Islamic gunmen in Somalia vow guerilla war.

Is this enough, or shall we go on?

The interesting thing about all this: the word *sin* is not mentioned once in these articles. Feel free to inspect your own local newspaper. See if you find the word.

But let's be fair. The word *sin*, like *love*, is hard to pin down. It is a *slippery* word.

The Bible has several Greek and Hebrew words for sin.

    Chata

    Avah

    Pasha

    Hamartia

    Adikia

    Parabasis

    Paraptoma

    Anomia

    Asebia

    Enochos

Theologians have lots of categories to speak about sin. Sometimes they sound like Bubba telling Forrest Gump how many different kinds of shrimp you can have.

    Original sin

    Individual sin

    Corporate sin

    Unpardonable sin

    Willful sin

Social sin
Domestic sin
Foreign sin
Mortal sin
Venial sin
High-handed sin
Sins of ignorance
Sins of omission
Sins of commission
Seven deadly sins

Plenty of sin to keep theological ink flowing for years to come.

But when you go beyond the theological categories, you find that common folk also mean a wide array of things when they say *sin.*

On any given day someone will pronounce that sin is
a stolen candy bar
a woman preacher
the science of evolution
the other political party
social drinking and dancing
the rumpled sheets of a bed shared with another man's wife
a mother puffing cigarette smoke into the house where her children breathe

a large pipe dumping sludge into the local
river
homeless people sitting around a
trash fire in a vacant lot between
two skyscrapers
militarism
the dismantling of affirmative action
depletion of the ozone layer
the end of inconvenient life in a
womb.

When we say *sin*, we mean many things. What is sin to
one is not necessarily sin to another.

But not to fear. There are plenty of opinionated people
who have solved the riddle of sin. They know how to fix
it.

The *moralists* suggest that we all just try to get along.
Use the power of positive thinking and behave better.
Pick ourselves up by the bootstraps and do the right
thing. God wants us to try harder.

The *educators* suggest that sin is a problem to be
solved in the brain. We need values clarification, cultural
enlightenment, and reformed thinking. Sin is solved by
degrees—the academic kind.

The *biologists* suggest that maybe sin is in the genes.

We have a natural proclivity toward either sin or sainthood. We need the sanctifying therapy of gene repair.

The *politicians* suggest that sin is in our social systems—and it is. Electing the right politician or political party is the key. If we fix society, we will eliminate crime, poverty, disease, and lots of other sinful ailments—and we won't.

The *psychologists* suggest that our behavior is understandable, predictable, and explainable based on what happened to us. We need therapy, and maybe some meds on the side. And maybe we do.

The *TV preachers* suggest that we need to touch the screen, demand that our demons depart, and send in $25 per month as seed faith money to affirm our healing.

Other religious folk have concluded that we're all just sinners. We sin every day in every way. We have sinned for centuries and always will, so why not become good at confessing and try not to hurt anybody along the way. We should lower our expectations about deliverance from sin and not feel so guilty. After all, we're only human.

These people are not all wrong, but being half right is not necessarily better.

INTRODUCTION

The Gospel writer, Matthew, must not have known many educators, politicians, psychologists, or religious leaders. Otherwise he would not have written something so utterly simple, yet so utterly stunning. The angel of the Lord is making an announcement to Joseph, the man who refuses to do what is religious—put away his wife for cause of adultery. The angel says, "Joseph, son of David, do not be afraid to take Mary as your wife, for the child conceived in her is from the Holy Spirit. She will bear a son, and you are to name him Jesus, for he will save his people from their sins" (Matt. 1:20-21).

What kind of solution is this supposed to be?

Jesus—fully human. I suppose that does away with the sin excuse that says, "Well, I'm only human." If Jesus is the full definition of being human, then sin is an intrusion into the saintly humanity that God created. Sin, therefore, is sub-human, un-human, anti-human, other-than-human.

Jesus—mortal, fleshy body, limited, weak, disease-able, decay-able, death-able.

Jesus—full of natural desires, hungry, thirsty, emotional, sexual, extroverted and introverted. Myers-Briggs-able.

Jesus—going through the stages of human development. Puking baby, inquisitive two year old (was he terrible at age two?), red-faced boy with a ball, puberty, first job, women, relatives, daily demands, inner pressures.

He is like us in every way, except sin. Why?

Some have focused on His virgin birth, suggesting that the absence of the male is the secret to sinless existence. They say sin is in the sex act that procreates. By skipping the sex, God skipped the sin and Jesus was born better than all the rest of us who were made the old-fashioned way. I would guess there are women saying "Amen" right now. Get rid of the sin-carrying males and the world will be a better place.

Hold on sister.

I don't think Jesus was sinless because Joseph was absent during the conception. Rather, I think Jesus was sinless because the Holy Spirit was present. The child conceived in Mary is from the Holy Spirit, the Spiritus Sanctus, the sanctifying, holy-making Spirit of God.

Jesus is God-breathed. He lacks the package of self-items:

Self-rule.

Self-will.

Self-gratification.

Self-indulgence.

Self-glorification.

Self-ways.

Selfishness.

Jesus understands himself not by separation from all other selves, but by His unique relationship with the Father from whom He comes. His identity is not rooted in self, but in relationship. He lives to please the Father. He learns obedience. He operates from the fullness of the Spirit in a fallen world. He is so holy that His life makes us uncomfortable enough to crucify Him. He penetrates our darkness with a holy flashlight, exposing everything shady about us. He speaks truth rather than words that tell us what we want to hear. He challenges all our idols of a god made in our own image. So we rid ourselves of this one who committed no sin, this one without guile or duplicity, this Holy One. And we remain sinful apart from Him.

What can wash away my sin?

An hour in the counselor's office?

Gene therapy?

My political party coming to power?

A master's degree?

The power of positive thinking?

Sending $25 to the TV preacher?

INTRODUCTION

Why not Jesus? He came to save us from our sin.

Me—sinless? Probably not. We live in frail bodies in a fragile world. Sin's claws are deeper into us than we know. Our own motives are more tainted than we know. Our own rationale is more stained, our own judgment is more impaired, our own righteousness is filthier—and our corporate sin is more pervasive—than we will ever know.

But Jesus knows us better than we know ourselves. He has vowed to fully save us from our sin. Completely. Totally. And I think He wants to start now. How far He gets before we are buried is a matter of obedience, openness, and circumstance.

I think we'd all agree that there is a lot of saving to be done to rid us of sin. I say we start letting Jesus save us. Now. Right now. Today. It will take a lifetime and a resurrection to get it done, but why wait?

ANGER

1

Deadly Anger.

What would cause a person to strap explosives around his body, walk into a crowded room, and kill?

What would bring a postal worker to the point of revisiting the site of his firing and take human life?

What would put a teenager on the street in prostitution?

What would send a college senior into a classroom with random murder on his mind?

What would cause a wife to take a knife to her husband?

What would cause a young man to endanger life by driving a car at speeds exceeding 100mph?

What would land business partners in court suing each other into bankruptcy?

What would cause a person to live looking into a bottle at the end of every work day?

Anger.

Yes, but a certain kind of anger—unresolved anger. And if you follow the bread-crumb trail backwards from the point of destructive anger, you will probably find unresolved loss. Something important has been lost and we are powerless to get it back, heal it, fix it, or protect it. And we are angry.

You know the lines—

> The person I'm in love with isn't in love with me.
> It's the coach's fault that I'm not starting.
> The doctors missed the clues. They are so inept.
> I deserved that promotion. But they had it out for me.
> This stupid job. It's their fault for moving us here.
> Simon doesn't know anything about music. I am an Idol!

We lost something and we are powerless to get it back. The loss of power makes us angry. Crime testifies to the fact. Rage pours from terrorists who see no other way to have the world as they wish it. The masses revolt violently. Spouses retaliate vengefully.

Anger is deadly. And like acid in a plastic jug, it destroys its container first.

Anger comes in many varieties.

> *Resignation anger*—My esteem is shot. Hurt me if you want. Use me if you wish. Trample me under

foot. Pain is better than nothing. At least I know I'm still alive.

Crock-pot anger—The lid is on but what's inside is steaming. And when the right temp is reached, somebody's gonna pay.

Blaming anger—It's their fault. I'm a victim. They are to blame.

Subtle, controlling anger—I'll never let anybody do this to me again, so back off.

Powder-keg anger—I dare you to push the button. The Incredible Hulk is going green.

Random anger—I'm not responsible for what I do. No one cared that I got hurt, so why should I care that they get hurt?

Follow the trail. The bread crumbs lead to loss.

In Eph. 4:26-27, Paul tells us to be angry and sin not. To this he pens an interesting warning: "Do not let the sun go down on your anger and do not make room for the devil."

I suppose the devil prefers the low-rent district of unresolved anger. He will go to bed with us, use our dreams as a rehearsal for what was done to us, and haunt our waking restlessness. He will get up the next morning and go to work on unresolved anger. By the time he is done in the kitchen, he has cooked up a stew of bitterness, spite, prejudice, backstabbing, gossip, abuse, insults, nerves, resentment, rage, tantrums, cussing, sulking, moods, and attitudes. He becomes the CEO of our perspective, and all reality passes through his interpretative grid. We open wide and swallow whole the stew that destroys. Before we know it, we are enemy-centered people. We see in every person remnants of the one who wronged us. Our defenses go up toward them. Our quills extend in self-protection. Our looks kill, and our words are daggers that go deep into their soft bellies. They never saw what hit them. They recoil from us. And the devil insinuates that they are our enemy. Our whole life is organized around being angry, and the devil is the daily chef of the stew we consume.

This anger is deadly.

But there is another version.

Un-Deadly Anger.
We are angry. And we have our reasons.
> Adults who should have been safe, but weren't.
> Parents who should have stayed married, but
>> didn't.

ANGER

Kids at school who could have been nicer, but
     weren't.
Bosses who should have been fair, but weren't.
A church that could have helped, but didn't.
A roommate who should have told us what
     everyone was saying, but didn't.
A person who should have stayed faithful, but didn't.
People who should have left our stuff alone, but
     didn't.
Institutions that could have flexed, but wouldn't.
Disease that could have landed elsewhere, but
     didn't.
Death that should have waited, but wouldn't.

We are angry. And we have our reasons. And those
reasons are the most reasonable reasons of all—to us.
So we are angry. Some of us know it. Some of us don't.

Anger is the emotion that tells us
     that we are not getting what we want or deserve.
     that our will is being blocked or frustrated.
     that we are losing someone or something very
     important to us.

Anger is that flashing red light on our instrument panel
     that says, "Pay attention! Something is wrong
     here."

ANGER

And the Bible has a very interesting two-word command
about anger: BE ANGRY!

Paul is explaining to the Ephesians the new life they are
being schooled in. He tells them they are no longer living
by the old lessons of self-centeredness, but by the new
way of Jesus-likeness. When God raised them from their
dead, old ways, he resurrected them into new learning.
In essence Paul says,

> Be angry, but don't sin.
> Be angry, but don't stay angry.
> Be angry, but don't room with the devil.

It appears that Paul assumes we will be angry. But what
matters is what we do with it and about it.

In Matt. 5, Jesus discusses anger in conjunction with the
Old Testament law about murder.

> You have heard that it was said to those of ancient
> times, "You shall not murder;" and "whoever
> murders shall be liable to judgment." But I say to
> you that if you are angry with a brother or sister,
> you will be liable to judgment; and if you insult a
> brother or sister, you will be liable to the council;
> and if you say "You fool," you will be liable to the
> hell of fire *(Matt. 5:21-22)*.

The consequences of anger seem to escalate in this text. We begin our anger with a warning about the liability of being judged and end it with a threat of hell-fire.

Anger is first an emotion for which we may be liable.

Then it becomes an insult. The word is *raca*. To pronounce it correctly, you need to spit from the back of your throat. To say it is to do it. We began with emotional feelings about a deed done to us, and now we have an attitude about it. We've slept on it, and woken with names for the person who did the deed to us. We hold them in contempt. Before we move to hurt them, we must pass judgment on them in our court of reasonable anger.

Finally, anger is a destructive deed. It is a deed used to say to someone, "Nabal" or "You fool." In biblical days, this was a curse. A curse was the opposite of a blessing. Where a blessing was words invested with power to give life, a curse was words invested with power to destroy. This particular curse assigned one to the trash heap of godlessness. The word is *nabal*. Say this to someone and you're headed to hell, or Gehenna, as the text records it.

I've been to hell. I went there several years ago with a group of college students. We were visiting Jerusalem when the guide pointed out the Valley of Hennom

(Gehenna). It was the city dump, the place where people took their trash and heaved it over the cliff and down into the valley. Earlier in Jewish history, the Ammonites had sacrificed their babies to the gods in that valley.

You may remember the description of hell—"the worms there never die, and the fire never stops burning" (Mark 9:48, cev). That's because worms were always eating the refuse and the public servants kept a fire going at the city dump to turn trash into ashes.

Gehenna—where everything worthless is taken and left.
Gehenna—where you put things that have no useful life
    left in them.

When you get to the point that the anger inside has moved from
    an emotion to be aware of
        to
    an attitude of contempt
            to
            a destructive deed . . .
    you are spent, used up, ready for the trash heap.
    There is nothing of worth or value left in the anger.

Most of us take our anger in one of two directions—outward or inward.

ANGER

Outward anger looks like road rage, yelling and screaming, a fist through a wall or a foot through a door, giving hand signals telling someone where to go, destroying property.

Inward anger is very different. It looks like obsessive worrying, biting your fingernails, depression, cutting, eating yourself to death, letting other people use your body, walling yourself in, suicide.

One of the clearest pictures of inward anger was painted in the movie, *Dead Poet's Society*. Neil was a college student who wanted to major in the arts. His father was a domineering man who insisted that Neil forget the foolishness of drama and instead, prepare to run the family business. Neil found himself torn between pleasing his father and following his dream. Though forbidden by his father, Neil won the lead role in Shakespeare's *A Midsummer Night's Dream,* and his performance brought the house down. His father, rather than congratulate him, took him from the cast celebration and drove him home, where Neil was given one more tongue-lashing. Late in the night, Neil sneaked quietly into his father's office, picked up a gun, and killed himself. That is anger turned inward.

Outward anger hurts others.

ANGER

Inward anger hurts us.

Either way, life is destroyed.

The good news is that there is a third option. We can take our anger Godward.

> Be angry—tell God.
> Be angry—don't sin.
> Be angry—vent heavenward.

God specializes in trash recycling. God takes the smoldering, worm-eaten trash of our lives and converts it to something useful—reconciliation, justice, peace. The anger is not discarded by God, but redeemed for useful purposes. Being a Christian does not eliminate our anger. It converts and transforms it.

Could it be that anger, yielded to God, shaped and directed by God, becomes the passion for redeeming the world? Could it be that redeemed anger is the energy we need to do something about a world gone wrong?

I wish I could be as angry as Jesus. And I'm not talking about the one-time temper tantrum He threw in the temple.

> I'm guessing it was anger that gazed into the Pharisee's eyes on Sabbath and saw the forbidding look—and He healed anyway.

ANGER

I'm guessing it was anger that stooped to the ground as people quoted scripture about stoning an adulterous woman.

I'm guessing it was anger that cast the devil out of a crazed man and into the town pork supply.

I'm guessing it was anger that stilled a storm.

I'm guessing it was anger that raised Lazarus.

I think the redeeming deeds of Jesus may have come from anger. He saw the world at its worst, destroying the people God loves, and He looked heavenward to the Father, asking, "What do you want me to do with this?" And the result was a passion for wholeness, justice, peace. The Spirit moved Him to act. He could not casually observe a world gone wild.

It makes me wonder if one day in England, William Wilberforce just couldn't stomach any more slave trading, and if he looked heavenward, asking, "What do you want me to do with this?"

It makes me wonder if Susan B. Anthony just couldn't stomach any more alcohol abuse.

ANGER

It makes me wonder if Martin Luther King, one day down in Birmingham, just couldn't stomach any more racial prejudice.

It makes me wonder if Charles Colson just couldn't stomach the spiraling plight of prisoners.

It makes me wonder if Nelson Mandela just couldn't stomach any more apartheid.

It makes me wonder if when we figure out what's in our craw, when we figure out what makes us angry, if we wouldn't be on the verge of discovering the passion for redemptive action. If maybe our calling is connected to our anger.

If there was more redeemed anger in the world, there would be less poverty, less discrimination, less character assassination, less abuse, less divorce, less pain. If there was more redeemed anger, there would be fewer battered wives, neglected children, religious frauds, power games, liars and cheats.

Christians are too nice. We swallow our anger too often. It's time we took it to God and figured out what to do with it. No need to waste things that can be recycled. Be angry—don't sin.

ANGER

Forest Gump loved Jenny. From childhood, they were bound in friendship. Jenny's father abused her. She took her anger inward and almost destroyed her life—drugs, alcohol, running, hiding, letting anyone use her body. She came to the brink of suicide. But Forest loved her. One day, as a seeking adult, she returned home. She walked down the road to her old house, long since emptied by the death of her father. The anger that she had turned inward suddenly erupted outward. Jenny began to hurl rocks at the old house. She threw every rock she could find, with every ounce of energy she could muster, and then fell in a heap in the road. Forest sat down beside her, took her in his loving arms, and said those profound words—"Sometimes there's just not enough rocks." In that moment, Jenny's life began again.

God painfully watches our attempt to resolve our anger, as we either throw rocks at others, or stone ourselves. God stands ready in any moment to take us up in divine arms, recognize the pain done to us, receive the raw anger into himself, and redeem it for good. Only God can do this . . . and God's people on His behalf.

Anger need not be deadly. It may be quite lively!

ENVY

2

Anastasia and Drusilla. These two give step-sisters a bad name. They are cold and cruel. They want to reduce Cinderella to cinders, rags, and ashes. They degrade her, demean her, and dehumanize her. They experience her beauty as emptiness inside themselves. They experience her quiet peace as something they lack. Her presence causes them the pain of self-awareness. They feel persecuted by the good in her. Not only do they want what she has, they want her to be without it.

There is a name for this—*envy*. And it is a deadly sin. Those who practice it will never know life happily ever after.

Of course, Cinderella isn't the only classic story about envy.

There's Salieri and Amadeus Wolfgang Mozart. Salieri, responsible and religious, begs God to let him compose the music of heaven. Instead the gift is given to an obscene brat who chases girls, giggles incessantly, and cusses backwards. Salieri is green with envy and cannot enjoy the life he has been given for envy of another.

There's Cain and Abel. God is more pleased with Abel's sacrifice. Crawl inside Cain's head and you can hear envy talking. *You've been robbed. This isn't fair. You deserve better. Abel gets all the breaks.* So Cain kills

Abel. The crime is murder. The motive is envy.

There's Ray and Robert, the Barone brothers from TV. "Ma always liked you best. Everybody loves Raymond." Poor Robert can't enjoy his own life for the shadow of this brother's favored status.

There's Joseph and his coat of many colors, which agitates the tar out of his 11 brothers. Joseph didn't do himself any favors by wearing it everywhere he went.

There's a shepherd boy who brings down a giant with a slingshot and becomes more popular than King Saul. Saul has slain his thousands, and David his ten thousands (1 Sam. 21:11, NASB). And Saul, full of envy, throws a spear to pin David to the palace wall.

There's mean old Herod who hears of a new baby born in Bethlehem. It torments him. Soldiers act on Herod's envy with their swords.

There's the elder brother stewing out in the backyard while the father hosts a welcome-home party inside for the prodigal son.

There are the two ancient merchants who compete for business face-to-face across the street. Their rivalry becomes so bitter that God sends an angel to end the nastiness. The angel appears to one merchant and says, "You can have anything you want in the world—riches, long life, many children, wisdom. Just know that whatever you ask, your competitor will receive twice as much. What is your wish?" The merchant narrowed his green, envious eyes and answered, "Make me blind in one eye."

Envy is classic in the stories of human perversion.

Under the microscope, envy is fatal.

It destroys our capacity to enjoy the life we have been given. We're always feeling robbed, cheated, unappreciated. We experience our own life as a lacking, an emptiness. As it reads in Proverbs, "A heart at peace gives life to the body, but envy rots the bones" (Prov. 14:30, NIV). We don't like our life. We want another. So we go after the object of our envy. We are driven to humiliate Cinderella, kill Mozart, best Raymond, exile Joseph, spear David, shame the prodigal, blind the competitor. Envy is a deadly sin, destroying our capacity to enjoy life.

We know how to act on envy. Sabotage the project of the person who got our promotion. Paint graffiti on their door. Key their new car. Campaign for their demotion. Roll our eyes every time they say something. Make them the butt of our sarcasm. Chip away at their reputation. Dig for dirt and spread it. Tell lies.

Garrison Keillor says that envy is such a creepy little sin that few will ever confess to it. He once wrote of a man whom he envied, envying everything from his possessions to his successes to even the unfortunate facts about his life. It was to a point of contempt, hoping mishaps and bad endings would come to each venture or attempt at success.

Of course, you've never felt that way about anyone, holy as you are. You're more spiritual.

Thankfully, I have a little sympathy from my friend in Ps. 73. He as much as confesses the creepy little sin of envy.

> I was envious of the arrogant;
>> I saw the prosperity of the wicked.

> For they have no pain;
>> their bodies are sound and sleek.
> They are not in trouble as others are;
>> they are not plagued like other people.
> Therefore pride is their necklace;
>> violence covers them like a garment.
> Their eyes swell out with fatness;
>> their heart overflows with follies.

ENVY

They scoff and speak with malice;
>loftily they threaten oppression.
They set their mouths against heaven,
>and their tongues range over the earth.

Therefore the people turn and praise them,
>and find no fault in them. . . .
Such are the wicked;
>always at ease, they increase in riches.
All in vain I have kept my heart clean
>and washed my hands in innocence
(Ps. 73:3-13).

This person can't enjoy his own life because he has his eyes on another. Yet he is a believer envying a wicked man.

Ever heard a Christian say
>*I could own a bigger house like them if I didn't have to tithe all the time.*
>*I could go play golf too, if I didn't have to teach the fifth-grade boys in Sunday School.*
>*I could have a bigger business if I were willing to break the law like my competition.*
>*I'd be driving a new car if it weren't for the church building fund.*

The followers of Jesus are not immune to envy. I suppose we expect a break or two, a divine edge on the others. After all, we give, work, care, volunteer, and sacrifice, whereas others just look out for number one. If our lot in life is worse than theirs, we feel robbed, cheated, unappreciated. And our envy is masked as religious martyrdom. Deep in the heart, we stop believing that God is good to us. We experience life as a chore rather than a gift, a curse rather than a blessing, a weight rather than a grace. Envy is the ongoing regret of the life we have been given.

Too many Christians are eaten up with envy, hanging onto God with one hand while using the other hand to clutch for the life of another.

Reality check. We are followers of the Christ who wanted only the life that came from the hand of the Father. He experienced life full and free. He wronged none, served all. He redeemed, healed, included, and forgave. Did we experience His presence as our emptiness? His grace as our lack? His fullness as our void? Did His life remind us of the life we wanted but did not have? Was it easier to kill Him than to face our hunger? Was it easier to kill the good than to admit our lack of it?

Envy seeks to destroy the good it does not have. Envy pounds nails through flesh into wood. Whose hands are you hammering? Cinderella? The gifted Mozart? The father-blessed Jacob? The merchant across the street? Whose life do you prefer to your own? Look again at the hands. It is your own that you are wounding. You crucify the life God has given you for envy of another. Look one more time. Someone has taken your place, gone to the place where you are dying of lack, dying of emptiness. *His* hands receive the nails. The same hands that extend to give you the gift of your own life. Stop hammering. Open yourself to the joy of your own life. Be thankful, even charitable. You are not robbed, you are rich. You are not cheated, you are cherished.

The Psalmist finally figured it out, life is a gift from God.
>I am continually with you;
>>you hold my right hand.
>You guide me with your counsel,
>>and afterward you will receive me with honour.
>Whom have I in heaven but you?
>>And there is nothing on earth I desire other
>>than you.
>My flesh and my heart may fail,
>>but God is the strength of my heart
>>and my portion forever
>>>*(Ps. 73:23-26).*

GLUTTONY

3

Food. The Bible begins and ends with it. From forbidden fruit in Eden to a sumptuous wedding banquet in the Revelation. What we do with food is a clear reflection of our relationship to God.

> God said, "See, I have given you every plant yielding seed that is upon the face of all the earth, and every tree with seed in its fruit; you shall have them for food. And to every beast of the earth, and to every bird of the air, and to everything that creeps on the earth, everything that has the breath of life, I have given every green plant for food." And it was so. God saw everything that he had made, and indeed, it was very good *(Gen. 1:29-31)*.

> Then the LORD God formed man from the dust of the ground, and breathed into his nostrils the breath of life; and the man became a living being. And the LORD God planted a garden in Eden, in the east; and there he put the man whom he formed. Out of the ground the LORD God made to grow every tree that is pleasant to the sight and good for food . . . *(Gen. 2:7-9)*.

The provision of food is the expression of God's creating activity. The interesting fact is that both the human and the food we humans eat come from dirt. The difference is that God breathed into our dirt the breath of life and we became creatures capable of relationship with God. When God breathed into our nostrils we became a living being—*nephesh*. The root of this Hebrew word is *throat*, a passageway from outside our body to the inside. It is this passageway through which all that sustains us passes—food, water, air. We are empty and need to be fed. We cannot retain our food or water or air; we need replenishing. We are open throats, walking thirsts, human breathings. Chutes. And God is the one who takes initiative to fill our emptiness. God is our provider, our feeder.

This is not the only time we see this relationship between God and people in scripture.

> In the wilderness, manna is rained down from heaven and water flows from the rock.
> The prophet Elijah is fed by ravens.
> The 4,000 and the 5,000 in the Gospels dine on loaves and fish, courtesy of the Bread of Life.
> In the communion meal, we are fed the body and blood of Jesus in the meal of remembrance.

This leads us to confess that food is good. Food is the provision of God, a gift of divine origin. Food is savory, tasty, delicious, pleasurable. My father-in-law often comments to the cook that the evening meal is musty—musty have more! And he extends his plate for the next installment.

When Adam and Eve ate, they were participating in a sacred event. God was the provider. They were the creatures needing help from outside. Eating is a sacrament of dependence on God. It is as mysterious as sex. It involves taste buds, smells, flavors, and food preferences. Eating is sensual. Adam and Eve knew it.

But one day, they decided to rebel against the dependent act of opening their throats three times a day. They wanted to be like God—to be the feeder, not the fed. Independent. They raided God's tree in hopes of shedding their dependent status. In that moment, the universe shifted.

This is not what God intended. To be fully human is to accept our neediness and hunger as a reminder that we are creatures, not Creator. We are meant to live in relationship with the one who feeds.

I've wondered if this was not the lesson of the 40 years in the wilderness. They needed to relearn the dependency thing. Without grocery stores, fast food on every corner, farmer's markets in every community, they would open their throats like birds in a nest, depending on God to feed them. God would send manna, quail, and water. And God would remind them of the place they were given—a land flowing in milk and honey, loaded with figs and pomegranates, rich in oil and wine, with grape clusters so large that men with poles would be needed to carry the fruit. This central story of Exodus has food on almost every page.

When we come to the New Testament, we find the same. The central story is Jesus. He is all about food. He tells parables about feasts and banquets and dinner guests. He takes bread, blesses it, and feeds crowds. He blesses those who hunger and thirst after righteousness. He says, "My food is to do the will of him who sent me" (John 4:34, NIV). He teaches us to pray for daily bread. He is accused of eating good food with bad people when He eats with tax collectors and sinners. They even call Him a glutton and a drunkard. His last meal with His followers is a Passover Seder. On the cross, He says, "I thirst" (John 19:28, NKJV). Following resurrection, He reveals himself at a meal to the two from the road to Emmaus. They recognize Him in the breaking of bread. When He meets with startled disciples in a closed room, the first thing He asks for is something to eat. Later He invites the disciples' fishing party to a beach breakfast.

Food is a biblical topic. Which brings us to gluttony.

The church has been awkwardly silent on the sin of gluttony. Most of us could use one hand to count the sermons we've heard on gluttony, sermons that were probably preached by pastors coming off a successful Weight Watchers stint.

Gluttony is a word rarely spoken. Its first cousin, obesity, is getting honorable mention due to the plight of American school children and insurance risks. We're in the opening phases of an all out societal attack on obesity. Like global warming, it is a sin that has been there for awhile, but is just recently given its due in the destruction category.

Are gluttony and obesity synonymous? Yes and no. Obesity can be caused by heredity, chemical imbalance, certain medications, disease, metabolic rates, the set point of your body, genetic factors, and psychological issues.

Girth and gluttony do not necessarily go hand-in-hand, either. You can be skinny as a rail and still be a glutton. Obese people are no more automatic gluttons than red heads are lustful, blondes dumb, or left-handers prideful.

Gluttony is about our attitudes toward food, the practice of eating it in certain ways, and the habits we associate with food.

GLUTTONY

Gluttony has three traits:

1. *Eating to fill an emptiness that cannot be satisfied by food.* We feel isolated, lonely, troubled, anxious. We want this empty feeling to go away, so we begin stuffing our mouths or throats (nephesh) with food. We eat until the brain releases mood-altering serotonin which numbs us like an emotional anesthetic. We self-medicate with comfort food. Some people fill this emptiness with sports, romance novels, pornography, video games, or work. We do it with food. And we usually do this alone, separating ourselves from the very people who might offer friendship and listening ears for our emptiness.

2. *Eating as an exercise of power.* The world is a tough place and we often find ourselves powerless to change our situation. We are offended, hurt, angry. So we eat—because we can. And no one can deny us or prevent us. It is one of the few things we can do when we want and how we want. We spoon mini-shovels of food from carton to mouth in a show of power. Afraid to face the things we cannot change, we eat. We may be denied many things, but not food. We are not needy, powerless, or dependent when we have food in our hands.

3. *Eating as a signal of bad theology.* We were taught wrong things about food and it shows up in our eating. We grew up as consumers whose highest goal in life is to consume all that we want. We do this without regard for others, because the one with the most wins. We've never learned better. We're bored with our meaningless lives and eating keeps us consuming and therefore, important.

With gluttony,

 food is our salvation and comfort.

 food is more important than people.

 food is an individual fixation.

 food turns us exclusively inward.

 food numbs our emotions.

 food gives us a false sense of power.

 food is consumed but not enjoyed.

 food diverts us from the life issues that need to be faced.

Shall we open the confessional booth? Could it be that at the core of our relationship with God, food has assumed a role that it was never meant to have? And if, in one direction, gluttony is food gone wrong, compulsive dieting may be food gone just as wrong in the other direction.

Compulsive dieting is every bit as much an idol as the Babylonian gods. It is the god of thinness and it is our national obsession. Its bible is the newest diet book. Its altar, the bathroom scale. Its prayer, counting calories. Its goal, to be noticed. Its motivation, shame. Its idol, the perfect body. Its temptation, carbs and calories and chocolate. Its sin, weight gain. Its virtue, self denial. Its miracle, liposuction. Its repentance, bulimia. Its reward, smaller sizes. Its temple, the spa. Its sacred vestments, petites.

Women are especially vulnerable to the gods of thinness because our society places recognizable value on being as thin as a stick. The public notice of this value is transmitted through cultural icons, models, magazines, store mannequins, and TV personalities. But the most influential culprits are peers—the subtle look, the suggestion, the weight loss of a friend can become enormous pressure to join the fad.

Isn't it ironic that the same culture that demands of women tiny waists also demands large breasts? The part of the body given to the feeding and nourishment of healthy babies becomes the focal point of the female body. We expect women to feed their babies but be underfed themselves. The woman's body is a nourishing body, with a higher fat-to-muscle ratio than the man. Women gain weight easier and take it off harder. Yet culture places them under the judgment of the gods of thinness. The result is that most women hate their bodies, the very creation which enables families to create children and nourish them in infancy. How do we manage to be filled with the creating love of God and hatred for our own bodies at the same time?

Many women turn to other saviors from size—anorexia, bulimia, chemicals, diuretics, laxatives, surgery. Anything to please the god of thinness. And sadly, the age at which these gods begin to rule the heart is slipping ever younger. Junior-high girls are now asking for cosmetic surgery as a birthday present.

It is time that the followers of Jesus declare that these gods are frauds. They come to steal, kill, and destroy. They take life and give hollowness in return. The thin god will turn one into a self-centered, narcissistic, self-loathing, showcasing, lonely, empty shell of a human body. The thin god will keep one dissatisfied with appearance, forever chasing the fads of weight loss. In the search for quads of steel, biceps of steel, triceps of steel, buns of steel, abs of steel, one gets a heart of steel, hardened in body glorification. Life becomes nothing more than a fashion show with a runway that starts at the front door every morning.

Check the list of symptoms:

> My worth is rooted in how I look.
>
> My energy is given primarily to looking better.
>
> I eat alone and rarely converse around a dinner
> table.
>
> I skip meals.
>
> I make meal choices based on the food rather than
> on the relationships.
>
> I either hate my body or I am overly proud of it.
>
> I judge obese people to be failures in life.
>
> I believe I can climb the social ladder if I just drop a
> few pounds.
>
> I play skinnier-than-thou games with friends.
>
> I believe my life would be richer if I lost 10 pounds.

Shall we open the confessional booth?

Gluttony and compulsive dieting are fatal attractions, deadly sins. But they do not have the final word on food. Jesus does. He came as a needy human, dependent on the food that came as a gift from the Father's hand. He ate to sustain flesh and blood, skin and bones, fat and muscle. He loved to eat. He loved feeding people. He rarely passed up a banquet or dinner invitation.

I imagine that Jesus' prayers of thanks were similar to the child who offered grace by naming every food on the table and explaining to God why she likes it. I can imagine Jesus chewing slowly, savoring bites, thanking the cook, remembering a good meal. I suppose Jesus even burped and asked for seconds of the foods He liked.

But Jesus knew that food was not the ultimate good. He had food to eat that could not be purchased at the grocery store. He knew that people did not live by bread alone. He knew that His food was to do the will of the Father who had sent Him. He knew that fullness was more than a function of food, that it takes a life pleasing to God to make a human feel right in the pit of the stomach, that our deepest longings and hungers are met in partnership with God.

How do we celebrate food as the good gift of God without letting it become our god? Two practices of Jesus are instructive—fasting and feasting.

Fasting.
Jesus fasted. Satan tempted Him to turn stones to bread. Not a bad thing for a Messiah to do in a world awash with hunger. But Jesus said no. He intentionally experienced hunger without satisfying himself, to remember that physical hunger is not the deepest of human needs.

Fasting reminds us of our need for God, our dependency on God, our humanity. Fasting heightens our sensitivity to God in a world that is bent on numbing us to spiritual things. Fasting causes us to feel in our gut the hunger of the world around us.

Don't confuse fasting with dieting.

Dieting is about my willpower over food.
Fasting is about my relinquishment of power to God.

Dieting is about human control.
Fasting is about human submission.

Dieting is about what I eat.
Fasting is about who I am.

Dieting is about losing weight.
Fasting is about becoming Christlike.

Dieting is about impressing people.
Fasting is about serving people.

Dieting is about shrinking my body.
Fasting is about surrendering anxiety over food and turning to God for life.

> Therefore I tell you, do not worry about your life, what you will eat, or about your body, what you will wear. For life is more than food, and the body more

than clothing. Consider the ravens: they neither sow nor reap, they have neither storehouse nor barn, and yet God feeds them. Of how much more value are you than the birds!

. . . And do not keep striving for what you are to eat and what you are to drink, and do not keep worrying. For it is the nations of the world that strive after all these things, and your Father knows that you need them. Instead, strive for his kingdom, and these things will be given to you as well *(Luke 12:22-24, 29-31).*

But Jesus did not stop at fasting. He also practiced feasting.

Feasting.

Jesus ate with people and opened His life to them at the table. I bet He was a great dinner guest, and will be an even greater dinner host at the meal to come. Those at His table feel welcomed, wanted, and worthy of attention.

History begins with a couple of greedy gluttons grabbing forbidden fruit in the garden, but it ends with the people of God from every nation and tribe gathered around a table, eating with gratitude and thanksgiving at the wedding supper of the Lord and His bride. The Eucharist of heaven is a feast of grace and mercy, with plenty for everyone. And no one ever need leave the table empty.

SLOTH

4

SLOTH

What's Sloth?

If it isn't a two-toed creature, what is it?

Sloth is
> hitting the snooze button repeatedly.
>> drinking straight from the milk jug.
>>> leaving dirty clothes on the floor.
>>>> a love affair with the remote control.

> never returning calls or writing thank-you notes.
>> leaving only two sheets on the toilet paper roll.
>>> falling asleep every night to late-nite TV.
>>> living for sports.

tenured professors coasting intellectually.
> troubled marriages passing up a marriage retreat.
>> knowing TV characters better than family members.
>>> preaching other people's sermons.

wandering the mall, killing time, mastering small talk.
> amusing ourselves to no end.
>> letting discipline slide.
>>> indifference.

wanting to live somewhere else all the time.
staying busy to avoid serious thought.
preoccupation with misery.
boredom in daily routines.

not caring.
inability to sustain interest in anything
challenging.
feeling overwhelmed, and therefore,
doing nothing.
sloppy, undisciplined thinking.

resignation from responsibility for others.
letting others make my choices.
going with the flow.
surrendering hope.

lethargy.
apathy.
spiritual amnesia.
a deadly sin.

That's sloth.

For weeks at a time we go through the motions,
never seriously attending to God, never focusing on
God, never turning ourselves over to God. The
thought that by such negligence we keep on

wounding the only being who loves us with a perfect and expensive love—these thoughts become bearable and then routine. At last we put them away and sink into functional godlessness. When we are in that state, God does not seem very real to us. So we do not pray. The less we pray, the less real God seems to us. And the less real God seems to us, the duller our sense of responsibility becomes, and thus the duller our sense of ignoring God becomes.[1]

So what's the big deal?

Sloth: Back to the Garden

Every deadly sin has its origin in Eden. The feeding cycle of the garden is simple: Empty. Full. Empty. Full. With the repetitiveness of a ticking clock, humans live their lives in cycles: Morning. Evening. Morning. Evening. Sleep. Work. Sleep. Work. The connection between creature and Creator is rhythmic. And the chief end of man is to worship God and enjoy Him forever.

Yet Adam and Eve want more. If they can transcend their humanity, they will not be bound to the cycle of human living. They can escape the routine. The snake tells them it is possible. Eat from the tree in the center of the garden and they can make their own arrangements. They can reinvent the wheel, which hasn't even been invented yet. Life can follow their whims and wishes.

SLOTH

They can be independent creatures, filling their lives with excitement on demand.

So they ate.

And they were still empty inside. So they began to stuff themselves: food, TV, X-Box, the latest Grisham novel, the South Beach Diet, the stock market, power shopping, sexual conquest, idol worship, Survivor—anything to fill the void. We've always been prone to destroying ourselves when left to ourselves.

Slowly, something begins to happen to us as we keep filling the God-shaped hole with stuff. We grow tired, cynical, weary, numb. All these momentary diversions and thrills no longer excite. An emptiness settles in and it won't go away. Despair follows. We no longer care. We no longer feel responsible. We no longer want to try.

Some deadly sins can be done in a flash. But we have to work up to sloth. Like cement, it takes awhile to harden.

Some say sloth finds us mid-life. Until then we're too busy chasing forbidden fruit. Such fruit must be tasted and digested several times before we despair of it. Sloth is the last of the deadly sins to arrive. That's why it is thought of as a mid-life sin. But then, I work on a university campus, and I've seen some rather young versions of this old sin. Just writing about it makes me tire and want to stop writing. What about you?—Do you feel heavy, weighed down? Let's go fill the void with a snack. Oops. Gluttony seems to serve sloth quite handily.

God's response to sloth? Daily routine. Adam and Eve are sent into a world of farming and child rearing. Those who have done these can vouch for their repetitiveness. Till the soil, plant the seed, weed the plants, harvest the crop, put the crop away, get ready for next year. Have a baby, stay up at night with the baby, feed the baby, change the baby, put the baby down for a nap, change the baby, feed the baby. Add to this the laundry, which mates in the closet while you aren't looking. It seems to never end.

We want magic fruit, miracle formula, instant fix, a change-your-life-forever seminar. God gives us daily routines. We came from dust, we farm dust, we eat food from dust which returns to dust by way of the public sewer system—all this until we follow the food we eat back into the grave. Dust to dust. Ashes to ashes. So goes our life under the sun.

No wonder the writer/philosopher of Ecclesiastes called it *hebel*. This is the Hebrew word for smoke, nothingness, vapor, hot air. Meaningless, that's what life is.

SLOTH

Smoke, nothing but smoke.
    There's nothing to anything—it's all smoke.
What's there to show for a lifetime of work,
    a lifetime of working your fingers to the bone?
One generation goes its way, the next one arrives,
    but nothing changes—it's business as usual
    for old planet earth.
The sun comes up and the sun goes down,
    then does it again and again—the same old
    round.
The wind blows south, the wind blows north.
    Around and around and around it blows,
    blowing this way, and then that—the whirling,
    erratic wind.
All the rivers flow into the sea,
    but the sea never fills up.
The rivers keep flowing to the same old place,
    and then start all over and do it again.
Everything's boring, utterly boring—no one can find
    any meaning in it.
Boring to the eye,
    boring to the ear.
What was will be again,
    what happened will happen again.
There's nothing new on this earth.
    Year after year it's the same old thing.
Does someone call out, "Hey, this is new?"
    Don't get excited—it's the same old story.

SLOTH

Nobody remembers what happened yesterday.
And the things that will happen tomorrow?
Nobody'll remember them either.
Don't count on being remembered *(Eccles. 1:2-11, TM)*.

It's easy to see why Adam and Eve didn't like the arrangement. Dependent life can be monotonous. Get up. Brush your teeth. Deal with your whiskers one way or the other. Bathe a body that won't stay clean. Feed yourself through one inlet and empty yourself through others. Gas up a car that will soon be empty again. Wash clothes that will need to be washed again. Drive the same road that you will return on. Fill out a report, again. Prepare the lesson plan that you will prepare for another class this time next year. Shine a light in an ear. Open the hood. Call a prospect. Open the store. Keep the assembly line running. Start the sermon.

Routine. Life is made up of routine. Sloth has it easy.

Bored with life, we begin to shirk our responsibilities and care less. We hate life in this armpit town. We resent the demands people make of us. We want to be left alone in our deserved apathy.

Enlarge our life? Get out some? Been there. Done that. Too tired to try. Go away, please, just go away. You are bothering me. What do I want? Excitement. Ecstasy. Fantasy. Fulfillment. A high. A buzz. Elevation beyond the daily routine. But nothing works. It's all smoke.

God's response? More daily routine. Because God will not erase our *nephesh*. We are made with the capacity to be repeatedly filled and emptied. We are replenished daily, with enticing eternity in full view. And God has chosen to meet with us, and to give us life, and to be present with us, and to complete us—in the daily routines.

The routines that bore us are the places where God has promised to meet with us. The routines we want to be done with are the places where God becomes flesh and dwells among us, full of grace and truth. Where we want instant excitement, God gives us our daily bread. "The steadfast love of the Lord never ceases, his mercies never come to an end; they are new every morning" (Lam. 3:22-23). Hope in the Lord, child, now and forever. Our path to an eternally exciting tomorrow is through the routines of today.

Ours is a God of pots and pans, lesson plans, common work, daily bread, care for the neighbor, care for the body. The things we wish to transcend are God's sacred meeting places. Sloth would just as soon skip the encounter. Sloth has already decided that no good thing can come out of responsible routines.

God is the beginning and end of our journey out of sloth. It begins when a light of hope penetrates the stupor of sloth's gloom. "I woke, my dungeon flamed with light. My chains fell off, my heart was free, I rose went forth and followed Thee."[2] Maybe that's how it happens. The grace that precedes our freedom penetrates the darkness of despair. The move to liberate us begins outside us. Sloth exhausts the capacity to try. We need saving, and we will not save ourselves. Because we simply cannot.

God, however, can. Because God is holy love, unstoppable passion. God desires for His creatures life that is . . . well, life.

> God has in mind not just what we should be but also what, one day, we could be. God wants not slaves but intelligent children. God wants from us not numb obedience but devoted freedom, creativity, and energy. That's what the grace of God is for—not simply to balance a ledger but to stimulate the spurts of growth in zeal, in enthusiasm, in good hard work, in sheer ridiculous gratitude for the gift of life in all its pain and all its wonder.

> In short, we are to become responsible beings: people to whom God can entrust deep and worthy assignments, expecting us to make something significant of them—expecting us to make something significant of our lives. We have

been called into existence, expected, awaited, equipped, and assigned. We have been called to undertake the stewardship of a good creation, to create sturdy and buoyant families that pulse with the give-and-take of the generations. We are expected to show hospitality to strangers and to express gratitude to friends and teachers. We have been assigned to seek justice for our neighbors and, wherever we can, to relieve them from the tyranny of their suffering. . . .

But we have also been called and graced to delight in our lives, to feel their irony and angularity, to make something sturdy and even lovely of them. For such undertakings we have to find emotional and spiritual funding from the very God who assigns them, turning our faces towards God's light so that we may be drawn to it, warmed by it, bathed in it, revitalized by it.[3]

This vibrant life of partnership with God is described in Romans. What seems a punch list for Christians is actually the opposite of sloth—it is a responsible discipleship, a Christlike life.

Love from the center of who you are; don't fake it. Run for dear life from evil; hold on for dear life to good.
Be good friends who love deeply; practice playing second fiddle.

Don't burn out; keep yourselves fueled and aflame.
Be alert servants of the Master, cheerfully
expectant.
Don't quit in hard times; pray all the harder.
Help needy Christians; be inventive in hospitality.
Bless your enemies; no cursing under your breath.
Laugh with your happy friends when they're happy;
   share tears when they're down.
Get along with each other; don't be stuck-up.
Make friends with nobodies; don't be the great
somebody.
Don't hit back; discover beauty in everyone.
If you've got it in you, get along with everybody
(Rom. 12:9-17, TM).

Sloth: Coming to a Church Near You

I have a sneaky suspicion that sloth has morphed in American spirituality. While transporting us into the same old despairing state, it gets us there by way of Christian amusement. We want the next religious buzz. Like a coding patient on an emergency room table, we are waiting for the next jolt of the twin paddles to stir our sacred emotions to life again. And the Christian market is now flooded with CPR—Christian Products to Resuscitate.

Have you read Left Behind*? Well, it's just out and it will leave you on the edge of your seat! Did you hear they're making a movie out of it?*

SLOTH

Our group is doing The Prayer of Jabez. *Everybody's reading it. You wouldn't want your business competitor to enlarge their territory into your market. Better pick up a copy!*

When I watch the Gaither videotapes, I feel like I'm in heaven. And that Mark Lowery is just the funniest person on the planet.

Our church is doing Hillsong Music now. Finally something that is scriptural and sing-able. What's your church doing?

Did you see Benny Hinn last week?

I'm going to Weigh Down Workshop. Want to come?

Our church is studying The Purpose Driven Life. *I'm on day 27 of finding my purpose. They give us stuff to do every day.*

Did you know that Amy Grant has an old hymns CD out?

We've opened a Christian spa at our church. It keeps us away from the fleshy joints in town.

SLOTH

Our youth group is doing a work and witness trip to Disney World this summer. We hope to reach all the kids that wouldn't go to poverty-stricken places.

In the upcoming series on the book of Revelation, I will be revealing the identity of the Antichrist. You will not want to miss one single scintillating sermon in the series, which is available on DVD for $49.99.

All the guys are headed to Promise Keepers again this summer. Wanna go? I hear the woofers and tweeters are bigger than last year.

Did you know that Sean Hannity is a Christian? I watch him for devotions.

Our church is doing seeker-sensitive services now. The old ones were just for Christians. Next week is Biker Sunday.

Listen to us talk. Not that these things are wrong. In fact, many of them are helpful. But the routine of Christians across the centuries has never been the latest religious fad or fix. It has been the routines of daily prayer, scripture reading, Sabbath rest, common worship, tithing, hospitality, and deeds of mercy.

I suppose we got bored with the old routines. The newer amusements offer a jolt of religious energy faster than the old methodical practices. And the church across town is sparkling and sizzling. People are leaving their old churches in droves to get in on the new thing in town. Any pastor who doesn't keep up with the competition will be preaching to empty pews.

As a pastor, one of my favorite gatherings was the Wednesday night study group. We met for three years together. The tables were round. Marilyn made sure there was good coffee and even better snacks. We filed in from routine work and caught up with news from friends at our table. During our first year together, we learned how Christians pray by praying the Lord's Prayer, one slow line at a time. Letting it sink in and go down deep. Amazing how long it takes to really understand "hallowed be thy name" (Matt. 6:9, KJV). The second year, we learned how Christians live, by studying and living out the Ten Commandments and Beatitudes. We spent three weeks on "thou shalt not kill" (Exod. 20:13, KJV). I've never thought harder about the death penalty. We talked about adultery, homosexuality, and lust. We wrestled with how to bless the very people who persecute you. These evenings were more than sound bytes on tough issues. We became responsible for our way of life. During year three, we worked on how Christians think, by studying the Apostles' Creed. Again, one small line at a time. For three years, this group of people showed up regularly, thought seriously, talked respectfully, and grew by leaps and bounds. In most churches, this would have been a three week sermon series.

Sloth will not sit there for this kind of serious thinking. Sloth will head down the street where goose bumps are free and the preaching is entertaining. And even there, sloth will watch others make music without contributing a single breathed sound. Too much to ask of sloth to participate.

I wonder what will happen when Christians eventually tire of the amusements that their churches dangle in front of them to keep them interested. When the spectacular becomes commonplace, which fruit tree will they try next?

I suppose you hear my concern for a church that abandons the classic spiritual disciplines. I am convinced that nothing can take the place of the routine patterns that God has given us. Christians are still made the old fashioned way—one habit, one practice, one day at a time. John Wesley knew that the sanctified life was rooted in more than a second experience. It was enabled by the experience of love expelling all sin and grounded in the daily disciplines of holy people. Holiness does not just happen to us. We practice opening ourselves to the transforming, sanctifying presence of God. Nothing can replace the daily routines of the Christian life. To expect Christlike character apart from routine Christian practices is . . . slothful.

---

1. Cornelius Plantinga Jr., *Not the Way It's Supposed to Be: A Breviary of Sin* (Grand Rapids: William B. Eerdmans, 1996), 195.
2. Charles Wesley, "And Can It Be," in *Sing to the Lord*, ed. Ken Bible (Kansas City: Lillenas Publishing Co., 1993), 225.
3. Plantinga Jr., *Not the Way*, 196-97.

PRIDE

5

PRIDE

It took a nightmare to get Neb's attention. The story is narrated in the Old Testament book of Daniel. The story begins with Neb narrating his own tale.

> I, Nebuchadnezzar, was living at ease in my home and prospering in my palace *(Dan. 4:4).*

Life was good. Neb had won the coveted prize of Mr. Universe as the most popular ruler of the most powerful nation on the planet. No one threatened him. Hebrew slaves appeared at the snap of his fingers. Life in the palace was organized around his desires. He controlled reality. His codependent yes-men stroked his ego, massaged his macho, and told him exactly what he wanted to hear.

But late one night while he was sleeping, another voice crawled through the unlocked palace window, slid under the dead-bolted doors, slipped past Neb's sentries, traveled up the winding spiral staircase, and penetrated the king's strategic defense initiative. The unthinkable had happened: Neb had a nightmare. It was a nightmare that even the wool over his eyes couldn't stop.

> I saw a dream that frightened me; my fantasies in bed and the visions of my head terrified me. So I made a decree that all the wise men of Babylon should be brought before me, in order that they

> might tell me the interpretation of the dream. Then
> the magicians, the enchanters, the Chaldeans, and
> the diviners came in, and I told them the dream, but
> they could not tell me its interpretation *(Dan. 4:5-7).*

He summoned them all: the FBI, the CIA, the IRS, NATO,
and PLUTO. But there was not a clue to be known. They
could not decipher the king's horrifying dream. Enter the
hero of the book, Daniel. We already know from earlier
chapters that he is uncompromising, he prays three
times a day, and he is totally dependent on God. His
name even says so—Daniel means "God is my judge"—
and Daniel only cares about one verdict.

> At last Daniel came in before me—he who was
> named Belteshazzar after the name of my god, and
> who is endowed with a spirit of the holy gods—and
> I told him the dream *(Dan. 4:8).*

Neb thinks he has Daniel in his back pocket. He
renamed the young Hebrew after his favorite god, the
one that gave him the Mr. Universe crown. To name
something is to have power over it. Neb assumes
ownership of Daniel. But we'll see about that.

O Belteshazzar, chief of the magicians, I know that
you are endowed with a spirit of the holy gods and
that no mystery is too difficult for you. Hear the
dream that I saw; tell me its interpretation.
Upon my bed this is what I saw;
There was a tree at the centre of the earth,
        and its height was great.
The tree grew great and strong,
        its top reached to heaven,
        and it was visible to the ends of the whole
        earth.
Its foliage was beautiful,
        its fruit abundant,
        and it provided food for all.
The animals of the field found shade under it,
        the birds of the air nested in its branches,
        and from it all living beings were fed *(Dan. 4:9-
        12).*

The king had dreamed of a magnificent tree, a cosmic
tree, a colossal tree. It stands at the center of the earth
and feeds all living things under its shade. Humans and
animals alike are humbled at the base of this grand tree.
Wonder what or who the tree symbolizes?

I continued looking, in the visions of my head as I
lay in bed, and there was a holy watcher, coming
down from heaven. He cried aloud and said:

PRIDE

"Cut down the tree and chop off its branches,
    strip off its foliage and scatter its fruit.
Let the animals flee from beneath it
    and the birds from its branches.
But leave its stump and roots in the ground,
    with a band of iron and bronze,
    in the tender grass of the field.
Let him be bathed with the dew of heaven,
    and let his lot be with the animals of the field
    in the grass of the earth.
Let his mind be changed from that of a human,
    and let the mind of an animal be given to him.
And let seven times pass over him.
The sentence is rendered by decree of the
watchers,
    the decision is given by order of the holy ones,
        in order that all who live may know
    that the Most High is sovereign over the
    kingdom of mortals;
        he gives it to whom he will
    and sets it over the lowliest of human beings."
This is the dream that I, King Nebuchadnezzar,
saw. Now you, Belteshazzar, declare the
interpretation, since all the wise men of my
kingdom are unable to tell me the interpretation.
You are able, however, for you are endowed with
the spirit of the holy gods *(Dan. 4:13-18).*

PRIDE

The king's life is going fine until a divine being with a McCullough chain saw comes ripping down from heaven with timber on His mind. The instructions are terse. Chop it down. Saw off the branches. Strip the leaves. Scatter the fruit. Move the animals. Leave the stump.

In the middle of Neb's description, the tree changes from an "it" to a "he." And the tree, which is now a stump, is in for a long run of bad: he will be rained on, eat grass, live among the animals, and lose the capacity of human reason—for seven long years.

That's the dream. Ominous and foreboding. And Daniel must have given it away with a winced look. Neb reassured him, "Give it to me straight, son."

Daniel swallowed hard. "King Neb, I can only wish this dream was about your worst enemy. But it isn't. It's about you. The plain truth is, you are the tree, and God says you're comin' down."

> The tree that you saw, which grew great and strong, so that its top reached to the heaven and was visible to the end of the whole earth, whose foliage was beautiful and its fruit abundant, and which provided food for all, under which animals of the field lived, and in whose branches the birds of the air had nests—it is you, O king! You have grown

great and strong. Your greatness has increased and reaches to heaven, and your sovereignty to the ends of the earth. And whereas the king saw a holy watcher coming down from heaven and saying,

> "Cut down the tree and destroy it, but leave its stump and roots in the ground, with a band of iron and bronze, in the grass of the field; and let him be bathed with the dew of heaven, and let his lot be with the animals of the field, until seven times pass over him."

This is the interpretation, O king, and it is a decree of the Most High that has come upon my lord the king: You shall be driven away from human society, and your dwelling shall be with the wild animals. You shall be made to eat grass like oxen, you shall be bathed with the dew of heaven, and seven times shall pass over you, until you have learned that the Most High has sovereignty over the kingdoms of mortals, and gives it to whom he will. As it was commanded to leave the stump and roots of the tree, your kingdom shall be re-established for you from the time that you learn that Heaven is sovereign. Therefore, O king, may my counsel be acceptable to you: atone for your sins with righteousness, and your iniquities with mercy for the oppressed, so that your prosperity may be prolonged *(Dan. 4:20-27)*.

PRIDE

Pride. We're not talking about a healthy sense of self-worth or a proper self-esteem. We're talking about deadly pride, the kind that is snobbish, patronizing, condescending, rude, impatient, demanding, unkind, cruel, insensitive, pompous, egocentric, haughty, vain, superior, arrogant.

This is the pride of Lucifer himself, the once-upon-a-time heavenly angel of light who decided that he'd rather play first fiddle in hell than second fiddle in heaven. His carnival mirror was bloated beyond reality and Lucifer thought himself too important to stand in the shadow of the Almighty. So he split.

Pride is so easy to see in others, yet so hard to see in self. It is especially easy to see in a junior-high daughter. She has life all figured out. She knows more than her stupid parents. They are an embarrassment to her. The world revolves around her. The sun waits for her to get out of bed every morning before it dares to shine. She should not have to wait for her turn in the bathroom. The family meals should be what she likes. Her favorite TV program trumps all others. The parental taxi should be at her beck and call to whisk her to her essential appointments. All telephone lines should be clear when her friends call. I think you get the picture. Perhaps you've known such a creature. She drove me up a wall! And then one day my wife explained to me why this junior highness got to me—"She's just like you, and it bugs you."

PRIDE

Easy to see in others, hard to see in the mirror. Others are egotistical, we're self-confident. Others are vain, we're well dressed. Others are arrogant, we're just right. Others are demanding, we're pursuing excellence. Others are snobbish, we're introverted. Others are conceited, we're secure.

Pride does a number on the spiritual retina.

Neb saw, but he didn't really see. He heard what Daniel said, but he didn't really hear what Daniel said.

> At the end of twelve months he was walking on the roof of the palace of Babylon, and the king said, "Is this not magnificent Babylon, which I have built as a royal capital by my mighty power and for my glorious majesty?" *(Dan. 4:29-30).*

Notice the location. Up on a roof. High and exalted. Looking down on everyone and everything. It might as well have been the Tower of Babel, built by self-made men, assuring themselves that a flood would not be able to sink proud humans the next time. Up on his roof, Neb looks up to nothing and down on everything. His words are "I" and "my." He is not proud because he is strong, wealthy, and mighty; he's proud because he is stronger, wealthier, and mightier.

PRIDE

Pride pits itself against others. It has to win, one way or the other. Pride is never caught gazing upward, because it can't imagine anything higher. Pride must have the first word, which defines reality, and the last word, which takes credit for the reality. Pride renders us unteachable, unreachable, unchangeable. Pride is deadly.

And it comes in many forms.

It looks like the 1970s Beatles comparing their popularity to that of Jesus.

It looks like the White House of the Nixon era thinking that the laws do not apply to them.

It looks like a professor leaving a faculty meeting more enamored by what he said than what he heard.

It looks like a Bible scholar who thinks that how he interprets scripture is more important than how scripture interprets him.

It looks like the personals section of the local newspaper where a woman wanting to meet a man advertises herself as "strikingly beautiful, possessing a rare balance of beauty and depth."

PRIDE

It looks like a preacher who nails everyone to the proverbial wall each Sunday, but never visits his own dark basement.

It looks like Carly Simon's song, "You're So Vain," in which she says her ex-boyfriend will assume the song is about him.

It looks like Neb on the roof, looking down, saying things like "my mighty power" and "my glorious majesty."

> While the words were still in the king's mouth, a voice came from heaven: "O King Nebuchadnezzar, to you it is declared: The kingdom has departed from you! You shall be driven away from human society, and your dwelling shall be with the animals of the field. You shall be made to eat grass like oxen, and seven times shall pass over you, until you have learned that the Most High has sovereignty over the kingdoms of mortals, and gives it to whom he will." Immediately the sentence was fulfilled against Nebuchadnezzar. He was driven away from human society, ate grass like oxen, and his body was bathed with the dew of heaven, until his hair grew as long as eagles' feathers and his nails became like birds' claws *(Dan. 4:31-33)*.

PRIDE

The old sayings are true.

Pride goes before destruction,

a haughty spirit before a fall *(Prov. 16:18, NIV).*

God opposes the proud,

but gives grace to the humble *(James 4:6, NIV).*

Why is God so hard on pride? Because we make good creatures but lousy gods. We are meant to be full of something, but when we are proud, there's no room for anything but egomania. When we elevate ourselves, we destroy people, places, and things. When we refuse to humble ourselves before our Maker, we saw off the branch that holds us up, we unplug our own resuscitator, we tie a knot in the feeding tube that nourishes our life. God loves us too much to ignore our pride.

When that period was over, I, Nebuchadnezzar, lifted my eyes to heaven, and my reason returned to me. I blessed the Most High, and praised and honored the one who lives forever. For his sovereignty is an everlasting sovereignty, and his kingdom endures from generation to generation. All inhabitants of the earth are accounted as nothing, and he does what he wills with the host of heaven and the inhabitants of the earth. There is no one who can stay his hand or say to him, "What are you doing?" . . . Now I, Nebuchadnezzar, praise and extol and honor the King of heaven, for all his works are truth, and his ways are justice; and he is able to bring low those who walk in pride *(Dan. 4:34-37).*

God can bring us down from our lofty pride perches— if He wishes. It seems though, that God has taken a different approach to our human pride. Rather than powering up on us, God has powered down. Rather than sending a holy watcher with a chain saw, God has come in the flesh. Born of a humble peasant girl, He comes to us. He takes up carpentry. He stays poor, washes feet, values the lowly. He sides with the weak, the rejected, the powerless. He lays down His life in humble service for the very people who climb on the roof to avoid the same. He refuses to grasp for the divine equality that theology says is His. God does not pound us from above, but serves us from below. Only when we bow down, does this God lift us up. And when He does, we boast of being graced by such a humble Savior.

The God who could have met us in terrifying nightmares has chosen to meet us in the humble Jesus.

> When I survey the wondrous cross
> On which the Prince of Glory died,
> My richest gain I count but loss,
> And pour contempt on all my pride.

PRIDE

Forbid it, Lord, that I should boast,
Save in the death of Christ my God.
All the vain things that charm me most,
I sacrifice them to his blood.

See, from His head, His hands, His feet,
Sorrow and love flow mingled down.
Did e're such love and sorrow meet,
Or thorns compose so rich a crown?

Were the whole realm of nature mine,
That were a present far too small.
Love so amazing, so divine,
Demands my soul, my life, my all![1]

---

1. Isaac Watts, "When I Survey the Wondrous Cross," in *Sing to the Lord*, 239.

LUST

6

The wisdom of Proverbs is street wisdom, often expressed in street language. If the Proverbs were in today's vernacular, they would be even earthier. I suppose this is because Proverbs are the assimilated collection of human observation. People watched people and surmised what they saw.

Four successive chapters in Proverbs deal with chasing women—two very different women. The headings of the sections give a sense of the alternating pulse of the editor.

> Warning on Adultery—Prov. 6:20-35, TM
> Dressed to Seduce—Prov. 7:1-27, TM
> Lady Wisdom Calls Out—Prov. 8:1-36, TM
> Lady Wisdom Gives a Dinner Party—Prov. 9:1-12, TM
> Madame Whore Calls Out, Too—Prov. 9:13-18, TM

We all chase something. Some lust after sexual encounter, others lust for wisdom. One is called wise. The other is called a fool. The saga of the fool is told in these words:

> Dear friend, do what I tell you; treasure my careful instructions.
> Do what I say and you'll live well. My teaching is as precious as your eyesight—guard it!
> Write it out on the back of your hands; etch it on the chambers of your heart.

LUST

Talk to Wisdom as to a sister.
Treat Insight as your companion.
They'll be with you to fend off the Temptress—
that smooth-talking, honey-tongued
Seductress.
As I stood at the window of my house
looking out through the shutters,
Watching the mindless crowd stroll by,
I spotted a young man without any sense
Arriving at the corner of the street where she
lived,
then turning up the path to her house.
It was dusk, the evening coming on,
the darkness thickening into night.
Just then, a woman met him—
she'd been lying in wait for him, dressed to
seduce him.
Brazen and brash she was,
restless and roaming, never at home,
Walking the streets, loitering in the mall,
hanging out at every corner in town.
She threw her arms around him and kissed
him,
boldly took his arm and said,
"I've got all the makings for a feast—
today I made my offerings, my vows are all
paid,
So now I've come to find you,

hoping to catch sight of your face—and here
you are!
I've spread fresh, clean sheets on my bed,
colorful imported linens.
My bed is aromatic with spices
and exotic fragrances.
Come, let's make love all night,
spend the night in ecstatic lovemaking!
My husband's not home; he's away on
business,
and he won't be back for a month."
Soon she has him eating out of her hand,
bewitched by her honeyed speech.
Before you know it, he's trotting behind her,
like a calf led to the butcher shop,
Like a stag lured into ambush
and then shot with an arrow,
Like a bird flying into a net
not knowing that its flying life is over.
So, friends, listen to me,
take these words of mine most seriously.
Don't fool around with a woman like that;
don't even stroll through her neighborhood.
Countless victims come under her spell;
she's the death of many a poor man.
She runs a halfway house to hell,
fits you out with a shroud and a coffin
(Prov. 7:1-27, TM).

And this is a description of seduction in ancient times. Today, we swim in a cultural ocean of blatant eroticism, sexual advertising, accessible pornography, seductive clothing, and body mania. Men are applauded for sexual conquest. Women draw attention by looking and acting seductive. Premarital sex is quietly becoming commonplace. Affairs are quickly excused. Janet Jackson and Justin Timberlake know how to shock and awe. Eminem sells lust. TV programs aim for the heat index with titles like *Desperate Housewives, Sex and the City,* and *Dirt.*

I asked a group of high schoolers to name examples of lust. They listed Paris Hilton, Britney Spears, Christina Aguilera, and the movie *American Pie.* I asked the same group to name examples of healthy, attractive relationships. They stared at me with a puzzled look on their faces.

I could pile on page after page about "how bad it is out there," but the truth is, it has always been bad out there. Except for the good ol' days. I think there were about three of them. We find them in Gen. 1-2, where the world as God made it is a sinless nudist colony in a sensual garden where a man and a woman live together in perfect fellowship with their Creator. There has never been better sex than in the garden.

LUST

So before we talk about the deadly sin of lust, we have to be perfectly clear—God is no prude. Bodies are beautiful. Pleasure is intended. Sexual intercourse is one of God's cherished gifts. Adam and Eve were blessed. They were naked and not ashamed. Sensuality is the making of the God who knit us together in our mother's womb.

And then, as in every sin, it all began to go wrong in the garden. They saw and seized the forbidden fruit, taking upon themselves the prerogatives of God. They raided God's tree. And the aftermath has cold words about human sexuality. They sewed fig leaves together to cover themselves—from whom? God? Or each other?

Fig leaves. I grew up in southern Mississippi, where the summers were so hot you could fry eggs on the sidewalk. We had a tall fig tree in our backyard and I was the most agile in the family at climbing it. When time came for fig picking, I put on long pants and long-sleeved shirts—in stifling heat. Fig leaves can leave you itching, chapped, and sore. I preferred the heat of the humid south to the rub of fig leaves. I will vouch for the fact that Adam and Eve really wanted to cover up in the worst way if they wore fig attire.

LUST

Why did their violation of God's forbidden tree cause them to cover their bodies? If they could violate God, I suppose they could violate each other. It was no longer safe to be naked in a fallen world.

Something fateful happened to love in the garden. The man and woman learned to objectify, use, conquer, manipulate, and lust after each other—with painful consequences. As the writer of Genesis puts it,

> He told the Woman:
> "I'll multiply your pains in childbirth;
> you'll give birth to your babies in pain.
> You'll want to please your husband,
> but he'll lord it over you."

> He told the Man:
> "Because you listened to your wife
> and ate from the tree
> That I commanded you not to eat from,
> 'Don't eat from this tree,'
> The very ground is cursed because of you;
> getting food from the ground
> Will be as painful as having babies is for your wife;
> you'll be working in pain all your life long.
> The ground will sprout thorns and weeds,
> you'll get your food the hard way,
> Planting and tilling and harvesting,

sweating in the fields from dawn to dusk,
Until you return to that ground yourself, dead
and buried;
you started out as dirt, you'll end up dirt"
(Gen. 3:16-19, TM).

Before—naked, not ashamed.
After—hiding, causing each other pain, cursed.
And so ends the good ol' days.

A word for the man. Adam, after the fall but before the
ejection from the garden, did an interesting thing. He
named the woman. This is the same thing he did with all
the creatures. To name something is to have power over
it in some way, to objectify it. Adam named the woman.
This is a profound change in the relationship. God had
given him the woman as bone of his bone and flesh of
his flesh. Now he views her as object rather than gift. He
uses her rather than shares the stewardship of the earth
with her.

When a man mentally manipulates a woman in the
pornographic studio of his mind, he is doing what Adam
learned to do: treating her as an object for his pleasure.
This is the sin Jesus was talking about in the Sermon on
the Mount when He spoke of looking at a woman with
lust in the heart. This is the sin of the young fool in
Proverbs who went looking for the woman of the night.

And why is this wrong? Because a man is destroying his capacity to love as God intended for us to love. When Jesus calls for us to avoid looking at a woman with lust in the heart, He is not trying to squelch sexual desire or make men into non-sexual beings. He is trying to save us from the fatal attraction that will cripple our capacity to love and be loved.

Jerry worked with me at the Alamo Plaza Motel in Nashville. We were both working our way through college. He was a student at Vanderbilt; I was a religion major at Trevecca Nazarene University. He worked the afternoon/evening shift, 3:00-10:30 P.M. I came on for the night shift, 10:30 P.M.-7:00 A.M. I would check in the late guests and do the evening transcript of the day's accounts. He would often let me know that if I needed him for anything, he would be back in room [pick a number]. He had checked in a guest and had gotten an invitation to her motel room after his shift was over. His attempt was to score. Many nights, he would return to the office with a woman's panties, his trophy for an evening of conquest. He proudly hung the conquered apparel in his locker.

I remember the night he came into the office and slumped on the couch. I was working on that evening's transcript and he began muttering to himself, meaning to be overheard by me. "I don't get it. Here you are a virgin, dating a great girl, never had sex and don't intend to until you're married. I've had more women than I can remember. You feel loved and valued. I'm miserable and lonely. I don't get it." It must have been divine inspiration that hit me in the middle of the night. "Jerry, I do get it. You are destroying your capacity to love. Every night, you practice bonding and breaking, bonding and breaking. Sexual intercourse is an act given by God to bind two people together in a covenant of marriage for life. It is a bonding act. When you bind yourself to a person you hardly know, and walk out of the room never intending to see that person again, you damage your capacity to love. You are learning to love and leave, not love and stay. It doesn't surprise me that you feel lonely. You've been doing nothing but using your fellow humans and treating women like conquests in a game. My goal for sex is to love and stay, to bind myself in marriage to one person and stay bound for the rest of my life. Call it boring. Call it conservative. I call it love as God intended for it to be."

I don't know if my motel sermon moved him or not. But I still believe what I said that night.

Jesus went behind the act of sexual escapades to the act of lust—the lustful look. When we can manipulate another person in our mind without their permission or consent, we are on the trail of objectifying people for our selfish purposes. We might as well give them a name, because we have begun the practice of using them for our purposes. This is dehumanizing. This is a deadly sin. It cripples relationships and destroys our capacity to grow as loving beings.

And what about seductive dress? The wisdom of the world is clear—if you want to get a man's attention, dress seductively. Proverbs would label this thinking as foolish. But it works. It does get a man's attention. And if you are willing to trade the loving intimacy of covenanted life for a gawk, why not? But I think women want more than this. Much more.

Relationships built on patterns of lust will erode like a sandcastle at high tide. They can't stand the ebb and flow of daily thoughtfulness. Thus the invention of casual sex and hooking up. No strings attached. Come and go as you please. No one gets hurt.

Wanna bet?

As a pastor for most of my life, I've dealt with young couples working toward marriage. I've heard all kinds of pre-marriage sexual stories. Hopes and regrets. The number one thing I wish I had in my pastoral arsenal is "take-backs." I've yet to hear, "I'm so glad I did it. It will make me a more experienced sexual partner." What I hear is, "If only I had that choice to make over again. Now I understand what it means to love someone completely, yet there's always going to be this ghost of the past in my bed."

The pattern of lust also works its way into marriages. In one of her columns, Dear Abby corresponded with a regretful reader:

> Dear Abby: Your response to "Wavering," whose husband wanted her to accompany him to a swingers' party, was right on. If she goes, not only will the dynamic of her marriage change forever, she may never regain her self-confidence.
>
> My husband talked me into the same thing in 1978, soon after our first child was born. I knew his first marriage had failed due to boredom, affairs, etc., and I naively thought it would keep him from straying. By the late 80s, I could no longer handle the lifestyle and the constant worry about AIDS. I finally got strong enough to say, "No more!"
>
> In 2001, one year short of our silver anniversary, I learned my husband had been having affairs throughout our entire relationship, with or without the parties. We have been separated ever since, but only recently has he admitted that he needs help and is finally getting it—too late for us.

Throughout our entire marriage, I never felt good enough because my husband always wanted something more. I didn't know until I began counseling, after our separation, that there was nothing I could have done to change his behavior or satisfy him.

I wish I could take back all the swinging. I am so ashamed. I have herpes, but thank God I don't have AIDS.

Please tell "Wavering" never to give in. Due to his sexual addiction, it's possible that her husband is already cheating.

—Fooled for Years

Dear Fooled: Thank you for the powerful testimonial. While some couples agree that swinging opens up new doors of adventure, I see it as slamming the door on what should be a precious, meaningful, mutual demonstration of love between husband and wife.

Regret is the cancer of life. You cannot change the past. I hope you are still counseling because it will help you to forgive yourself for your mistake.

A woman will never be loved the way her soul longs to be loved by following the path of lust. Sex should be fun, playful, responsive, aggressive, exciting—but most of all bonding. God intends that we celebrate the union of one life to another in an act of self-giving love. Marriage built on lust is fickle, selfish, immature, and egocentric.

Lust demands more, but gives less. Lust wants a body to practice on; love asks for a life partner to be faithful to. Lust turns people into objects to be consumed. No wonder Adam and Eve reached for fig leaves. No wonder Jesus suggested the removal of the lusting eye (figuratively).

> You know the next commandment pretty well, too: "Don't go to bed with another's spouse." But don't think you've preserved your virtue simply by staying out of bed. Your heart can be corrupted by lust even quicker than your body. Those leering looks you think nobody notices—they also corrupt.
>
> Let's not pretend this is easier than it really is. If you want to live a morally pure life, here's what you have to do: You have to blind your right eye the moment you catch it in a lustful leer. You have to choose to live one-eyed or else be dumped on a moral trash pile. And you have to chop off your right hand the moment you notice it raised threateningly. Better a bloody stump than your entire being discarded for good in the dump *(Matt. 5:27-30, TM)*.

If we wish to use, manipulate, and hurt someone, why not begin with ourselves? But no one in their right mind would do such a thing. If we refuse to take destructive liberties with our own body, why not extend the same regard to other bodies? This is loving the neighbor as we love the self. This is how love was in the good ol' days, and how it will be again in the kingdom of God.

GREED

7

Greed.

In 1923, nine of the world's wealthiest men gathered in the Edgewater Beach Hotel in Chicago. The group was comprised of

> The president of the world's largest steel company.
>
> The president of the world's largest utility company.
>
> The president of the world's largest gas company.
>
> The world's greatest wheat speculator.
>
> The president of the New York Stock Exchange.
>
> A cabinet member of the president of the United States.
>
> The biggest bear on Wall Street.
>
> The head of the world's largest monopoly.
>
> The president of the Bank of International Settlements.

The supreme masters of world finance had gathered. You would imagine that these men were set for life and would enjoy their days upon the earth.

Fast forward 25 years to 1948.

> Charles Schwab died bankrupt after living on borrowed money his last five years.
>
> Samuel Insull died penniless in another country, having been on the run from the law.
>
> Howard Hopson was insane.
>
> Arthur Critten was insolvent.

GREED

Richard Whitney was just released from Sing Sing
Prison.

Albert Fall was pardoned from prison so he could
die at home.

Jesse Livermore committed suicide.

Leon Fraser committed suicide.

Ivan Kreuger committed suicide.

The men who had once mastered money had somehow
suffered a fate under its curse. Whether it was losing it in
the Great Depression, or misusing it, or falling prey to its
power over reason, their lives unraveled.

I wonder if any of the nine ever considered Paul's
wisdom to young Timothy.

A devout life does bring wealth, but it's the rich
simplicity of being yourself before God. Since we
entered the world penniless and will leave it
penniless, if we have bread on the table and shoes
on our feet, that's enough. But if it's only money
these leaders are after, they'll self-destruct in no
time. Lust for money brings trouble and nothing but
trouble. Going down that path, some lose their
footing in the faith completely and live to regret it
bitterly ever after (1 Tim. 6:6-10, TM).

These were the words of Paul to a young man. Greed
begins early, and seldom takes its foot off the pedal until
we are in the grave.

GREED

Somewhere in the world right now, advertisers are planning for the Christmas assault. They no longer wait until the Thanksgiving table is cleared. Around Labor Day they begin telling us to get a jump on the Christmas shopping. I must confess some sarcasm about the commercialism of Christmas. I believe in going to the mall once a year, for about 15 minutes. If I were the American prototype, the country would be in a serious recession. Merchants would be closing their stores in droves. I hate to shop. And walking the mall to look at what's there is my idea of torture. My wife, on the other hand, is the patron saint of merchants. And I find the gift-giving scene on Christmas morning a joyous occasion, due largely to her shopping excursions on behalf of our whole family.

My earliest recollection of Christmas wishing revolves around the thick Sears and Roebuck Catalogue. Dad worked for Sears. We got a good discount on everything Sears sold. He would bring copies of the catalogue home in the fall and we three kids felt like we three kings as we sat drooling over the pages. We had to decide what we wanted and prioritize it by placing a number beside the item. My most difficult year was age 13. I was aging into the big ticket years when things like guitars, miniature race car tracks, hunting equipment, and stereos were enticing me to pick them. My parents were wise to limit my choices. I wanted them all. I wanted them bad. I wanted them now.

GREED

The lure book is no longer a catalogue. It is commercials during the cartoons that our kids watch while we are busy doing other things. It is advertising that sneaks past our watchful sentry and entices our child with irresistible merchandise. I call this the mauling of young souls. And they don't even have to go to the mall to be mauled.

Do I begrudge children their toys? Are you kidding? I have grandchildren now, and I want to be the one to race to the store and get them what they want, mostly because their grandmother is fast at that job.

Do I begrudge stores their sales? As a pastor for most of my life, my salary has come from good business people who made profit and dropped a tithe in the offering plate. To wish them not to profit would be my own financial demise.

But this rush to extravagance is where "gotta have it" and "can't live without it" begins. This is where greed is a seed planted deep in the innocent soul of a child. If a child is schooled in whining, pouting, and getting, greed is well on the way to doing its deadly work.

GREED

During teen years, the game gets nastier. Theirs is a cruel world of judgment based on brand and taste. Are your tennis shoes the right ones? Do you have the latest CD and the right technology to play it on? Can you amuse yourself with portable devices? Are you wearing the right things and are you wearing them the right way? The fragile esteem of a teen hangs on gaining acceptance in a world of peers that often destroys. Many teens are not capable of withstanding the assault and their greed is attached to survival in the junior-high jungle. They don't have the capacity to figure this game out. The deadly sin is subtly at work making promises about popularity.

Greed at college? Every freshman gets credit card applications in the mail. I've seen the splashy brochures. The messages suggest that their lives are being minimized by lack of goods and that college is about living life to the max. *No need to wait, you can have it now. Enjoy your college years. You have a lifetime to pay it back. Be the person on campus you want to be. Join the human race. Get a credit card!* But not one brochure mentions that educational debt is piling up, and government loans will one day be due, and at the present moment, that student DOESN'T HAVE A JOB. Can you hear my decibel increase?

GREED

The possession of a credit card is now the equivalent of having a driver's license. It is the right of every American! (Sarcasm again. Sorry.) Just as Adam and Eve reached for the forbidden fruit, we grab the card and consume our hearts desires. We are the MASTER in CHARGE. We are AMERICANs who know how to EXPRESS ourselves. We can DISCOVER who we are. We are the heirs of Caesar who stated "veni, visi, VISA"—"I came, I saw, I charged."

Denise and I have done our share of pre-marriage counseling. Call us old-fashioned, but we have encouraged couples to begin their married life without a credit card. We espouse the envelope system. Cash your check; place a set amount of budgeted money in an envelope, dividing for groceries, gas, entertainment, clothes, haircuts, vacation, etc. Pay the mail bills by check, but everything else by cash. Inconvenient? Certainly. But the value is in learning to live on what you make, and saving ahead for things like vacations and major purchases. If the envelope is empty the answer is no. We did this for years. It forms a principle of careful stewardship instead of indulging the appetite.

It takes years to make a person deeply greedy. By the time they are formed, they do not realize the shaping work done by a deadly sin. It seems natural to them as the world cheers them on and sends another credit card application in the mail. The conscience is easily conformed to greed in a consuming society.

God started working on the greed of His people as soon as they cleared the Red Sea. Wilderness was their training ground for life. They were totally dependent on God. No crops. No fast food restaurants. No Kroger's or Wal-Mart. Just God. He gave them manna in the morning and quail in the evening. The instructions were simple. Gather only what you need. Some got greedy and began to stockpile the heavenly groceries, only to discover maggots in their manna. The lesson was simple. Learn to live from the hand of God. Go out every day and work for what He gives you. On the sixth day, gather enough for the seventh day. Enough is enough. Don't stockpile. Don't get greedy.

Now to the point. Greed is a deadly sin because it destroys our capacity to trust God. It suggests that we can secure ourselves and please ourselves by the possession of things rather than in obedient relationship with God. It destroys our concern for our neighbor and for their "enough." Greed makes us small.

Small like Ebenezer Scrooge. He has become the personification of greed in *A Christmas Carol.* While Tiny Tim is blessing everyone, Scrooge is bilking everyone. This master of misery is not only greedy; he has lost his capacity to behold the humans that frequent his life every day. Greed blinds before it kills.

Scrooge reminds us of the one called fool in the parable of Luke 12:16-21.

> Then he told them this story: "The farm of a certain rich man produced a terrific crop. He talked to himself: 'What can I do? My barn isn't big enough for this harvest.' Then he said, 'Here's what I'll do: I'll tear down my barns and build bigger ones. Then I'll gather in all my grain and goods, and I'll say to myself, Self, you've done well! You've got it made and can now retire. Take it easy and have the time of your life!' Just then God showed up and said, 'Fool! Tonight you die. And your barnful of goods— who gets it?' That's what happens when you fill your barn with Self and not with God" (TM).

This man was an early forerunner of Scrooge. Both believed in storing up for self. Both believed that life consists in possessing. Both were unconcerned for the neighbor. Both were stingy. Yet God intersects old Scrooge with angels of mercy who show him the past which shaped him. He went back in time to see what he had done to people along the way, people who had tried to love him. He went forward in time to see the consequences of his character. And he was given eyes to see the present moment in the Cratchit home, and the chair that would soon be empty. And he is changed. He did not change because he figured things out; he changed because he saw a possible future.

Can we? In a consuming world, can we imagine ourselves unplugged from greed? Is there a spiritual laxative that can loosen the constipation of stuff that clogs our soul? Stuff that is consumed but never passes through our hands. Stuff that clutters our lives like trinkets in a musty attic.

Greed is the anger that believes we have the right to posess stuff.
Greed is the envy of those who have stuff.
Gree is the gluttony of stuff.
Greed is sloth that becomes a thoughtless consumer.
Greed is the pride of having stuff.
Greed is the lust for stuff.

Is there any other way to live?

I know of a family that made a commitment to support several poor children in Haiti. A little more than $100 dollars a month was sufficient to feed, clothe, and educate five orphan children who otherwise would have no hope. In order for the family to carry out its commitment, there were sacrifices to be made. The children had to forego some of the things that many of their friends took for granted. They rode secondhand bicycles and sometimes their Christmas presents did not compare favorably with what their friends got. The family, nevertheless, stayed with their commitment for almost a decade.

One day the father of this family came home with some exciting news. His company was sending him to Haiti for a week to care for some business matters. Because his way would be paid by his company, he would be able to take his family along, provided they travel in the most economical way possible. The family was thrilled with the possibility of meeting the five children whom they had supported for such a long time.

The second day they were in Haiti, the family hired a jeep and drove out to the village where their young friends lived. The children, who were now teenagers, had been told of the visit and looked forward eagerly to the day when they would meet those who had done so much for them. The American family traveled for hours, but their tiredness did not detract from the joy they experienced when they arrived at their destination.

The five young people whom they had supported stood waiting in front of their school. They had been there since the early morning waiting to meet their American friends. As soon as the jeep stopped in front of the school, the five Haitian teenagers ran to it with happy excitement. The two American children bounced out of the jeep and into their arms and there followed a quarter-hour of glorious hugging. Despite the language barrier, the young people communicated their affection for each other. At the end of that special day there was an unplanned ceremony in which the Haitian children gave to their American friends Christmas tree ornaments they themselves had made out of twigs and sisal. After a long and affectionate good-bye, the Americans got back into their jeep to return to Port-au-Prince.

On the way to the capital city, the two children sat in pensive silence. Their silence seemed so strange and puzzling that their father asked what was wrong. "Oh, nothing's wrong," answered his daughter. "I was just thinking that there was nothing we could have done with our money over the last ten years that would have made us happier than we are right now."[1]

Un-greed.

We began in a garden where God provided everything we would need for a rich and full life. Everything was at our fingertips—food, air, work, relationship, love, beauty, conversation, sexual joy, creative engagement, nature. Nothing was lacking. And in this exquisite setting, God was as near as daily conversation. No limits were set, except for one. No requirements were placed on us, except for one.

"Everything in the garden," God said to us, "everything is yours to enjoy. But this tree in the center of the garden is mine and mine alone. You are not to take from it. By respecting what is mine, you will honor me as Creator and Lord."

Tithing began in the garden. It is the act of recognizing God as Creator and Lord by respecting that which is God's and God's alone. It is an act of worship. We take the first 10th of all we earn and hold it up before God each week. We are saying, "This belongs to you, along with everything else you have given us. We are stewards, not owners. And you have asked that we return this tithe to you as an act of respect and reverence. In this tithe we submit our entire life to you, offering thanks for the provision of our needs, and affirming our partnership with you in the care of all creation."

In the garden, we raided God's tree. We took what belonged to God. We fell captive to the avarice that cannot live within boundaries. We became greedy.

Much later in our story, the people of Malachi's day were

doing the same thing again. They were giving God all the sick, diseased, scrawny animals as a sacrifice of devotion. They were treating God like a trash can. He got what they no longer needed or wanted. And, in effect, God said to them, "You're raiding my tree again."

Across the years, I've heard many people opt out of tithing because it is Old Testament law, and we all know that, in Christ, the law has been abolished and we live under grace, not law—or at least that's how they rationalize it. Yes, tithing is found in the Old Testament law, and yes, much of the cultural law has been superseded or fulfilled in Christ. But tithing is rooted not in law, but in the opening narrative of creation.

We also see it early in Abraham's journey when he gives a 10th of the loot from a raiding excursion to a priest named Melchizedek. This was a long time before Moses came down the mountain with stone tablets in his hands and a long list of dictated law in his back pocket. Tithing is rooted in the narrative of our creation. Jesus has never abolished or done away with the practice of respecting that which belongs to God. He fulfills this act by enabling us to offer ourselves totally to God for the sanctification and hallowing of our entire lives. What better practice to begin with than to humbly place the tithe in an offering plate and say, "You are God and I am not. All that I have belongs to you. I return this 10th as an act of respect and worship. I cannot secure myself in this world. The ability to work and provide for myself and those I love comes from you. Grant me wisdom to use the remaining 90 percent as a good and wise steward."

Greed will throw a tantrum like you've never seen before. But eventually, it will give way to the practice of un-greed, or generosity. Enjoy tithing. God loves a cheerful giver.

---

1. Henry Fairlie, *Seven Deadly Sins Today* (Notre Dame: University of Notre Dame Press, 1978), 144-45.

CONCLUSION:
A LIFE OF SANCTITY

Are you odd enough to be a Christian? In my early years as a follower of Jesus, I sought to escape the oddness of Christianity. Most of the people in my small-town holiness church were not the winsome models of faith that I felt would cause the whole city to come flocking to the sanctuary doors asking to belong to us. I secretly hoped that none of my high-school friends would ask to come to our church because the people at my church were peculiar; they were odd.

One lady requested prayer for characters on a soap opera. Another showed hospitality by inviting the whole congregation to a chitterling fry—more correctly pronounced "chitlin." (If you don't know, don't ask.) People brought their guitars to church hoping to be asked to sing. Others hoped they wouldn't.

Odd.

I was convinced that when I grew up to be a pastor, I'd have a congregation with a different caliber of people in it, and town folk would flock to the sanctuary doors asking to belong to us, because we were more . . . like them.

CONCLUSION

I was wrong. Christians have grandly succeeded at becoming more like the world, less odd, much less peculiar. And in the process, have become marginal at best, unnecessary at worst. We've lost our odd ways.

I suppose "odd" is a strange synonym for holy. To say that God is holy is to say that God is not like anything, any created thing. God is in a category that has nothing else in it. Holiness is definitively odd. But it isn't an attribute of God. It isn't a word in the same category as faithful, sovereign, or merciful. It is a unique word that says there is no other one in whom holiness can be found. Anything that is holy is holy because God is reflected in or through it. Only God can "holify" people, places, and things. God's faithfulness is holy faithfulness because there is no other faithfulness like it. God's sovereignty is holy sovereignty because there is no other sovereignty like it. God's mercy is a holy mercy because there is no other mercy like it.

Holiness is the biblical word for the unique likeness of God.

First Peter. It's a letter in the New Testament. It is written to folk who have fallen in love with God and become loyal to the ways of Jesus. They were once cultural insiders, no different than anyone else you'd see on the street. But now, their new way of life has distinguished them, made them a bit odd. And the world isn't going easy on them. The have been slandered, ridiculed, excluded. Who knew that their faith would ever cost them this? Would they have courage to be considered odd because of God?

So Peter wrote to them.

> Therefore prepare your minds for action; discipline yourselves; set all your hope on the grace that Jesus Christ will bring you when he is revealed. Like obedient children, do not be conformed to the desires that you formerly had in ignorance. Instead, as he who called you is holy, be holy yourselves in all your conduct; for it is written, "You shall be holy, for I am holy." If you invoke as Father the one who judges all people impartially according to their deeds, live in reverent fear during the time of your exile. You know that you were ransomed from the futile ways inherited from your ancestors, not with perishable things like silver or gold, but with the precious blood of Christ, like that of a lamb without defect or blemish. He was destined before the foundation of the world, but was revealed at the end of the ages for your sake. Through him you have come to trust in God, who raised him from the dead and gave him glory, so that your faith and hope are set on God. Now that you have purified

your souls by your obedience to the truth so that you have genuine mutual love, love one another deeply from the heart. You have been born anew, not of perishable but of imperishable seed, through the living and enduring word of God *(1 Pet. 1:13-23)*.

Rid yourselves, therefore, of all malice, and all guile, insincerity, envy, and all slander. Like newborn infants, long for the pure, spiritual milk, so that by it you may grow into salvation—if indeed you have tasted that the Lord is good. Come to him, a living stone, though rejected by mortals yet chosen and precious in God's sight, and like living stones, let yourselves be built into a spiritual house, to be a holy priesthood, to offer spiritual sacrifices acceptable to God through Jesus Christ *(2:1-5)*.

But you are a chosen race, a royal priesthood, a holy nation, God's own people, in order that you may proclaim the mighty acts of him who called you out of darkness into his marvelous light. Once you were not a people, but now you are God's people; once you had not received mercy, but now you have received mercy *(2:9-10)*.

Do you hear what Peter is doing here? He is reminding them of their unique identity as God's blood-redeemed people. He is reminding them of God's investment in them through the death of Jesus. He is telling them who they are—the holy people of God.

This text is one that I memorized years ago in the old King James Version, written in Elizabethan English. But the phrase I've remembered most is the one in chapter two verse nine where Peter tells them they are God's own people or God's prized possession. But the old KJV calls them God's "peculiar people."

This word comes from a Hebrew expression found in Exod. 19 and Deut. 14 where God tells the people that if they will obey his commands they will be his prized possession, his peculiar people. The word is *segulla*, and it refers to a king's treasure—all the stuff that other rulers have given him as gifts of friendship and all the stuff he has collected or captured because of his sovereignty. It's the word for the bling around his throne that impresses the daylight out of anyone who comes to see him. When a visiting ambassador stops in for a royal visit, the ambassador is blown away by king's possessions. This dude must have lots of friends or hold huge power to have all this.

God says that when we live as His holy and obedient children, we are His royal treasure, His prized possession, His *peculiar* people. We are the representation of His holiness to all who look to Him.

CONCLUSION

What does it mean for us to be holy as God is holy? It means that because of the life of Jesus lived through us by the power of the Holy Spirit in us, we are recognizably, visibly, substantially different from the world we live in. We are odd in a different sort of way. Odd like God.

But it is important not to leap to the wrong conclusions about this oddity.

It is not an oddity that rages at the world and its wrongs. It is not an oddity that takes our marbles home in a sulking retreat into our private, protected, holy castles and away from the world.
It is not an oddity that decides to get enough Christians to vote for the same guy or girl so we can take over the government and be in power.
It is not an oddity that competes with the world for the most money, sex appeal, idol status, or fame in order to prove that we are just as good as them.

It is an oddity that we are rooted in likeness to Jesus. And this oddity cannot be reproduced by those given to a life of sin.

You see, sin isn't really impressive. Anybody can do it. Any sin is within reach of any human who puts his or her mind to it—or better yet, any human who simply lives outside of a relationship with God. Sin is mass produced by amateurs. You can find it anywhere, cheap.

Take the 7 deadly sins.
Anger is our response to loss or threat or hindrance.
Envy is a signal that we deserve as good as they got and we won't be happy until we gain or they lose.
Gluttony is filling our emptiness with whatever it takes to stuff and numb.
Sloth is our right to do or not to do as we please without being nagged.
Pride explains that your life is meant to be centered on me and I won't settle for anything less.
Lust is routinely marketed and bodies do what bodies choose to do.
Greed is culturally expected in a consuming world.

These sins are not impressive. Destructive? Yes. Impressive? No.

What is impressive is holiness—because it is so rare, so odd, so uncommon in a world of sin.

Instead of anger, imagine a people who turn their passion into justice and peace-making.
Instead of envy, imagine a people who actually rejoice in another's good fortune rather than being lessened by it.
Instead of gluttony, imagine a people who actually

practice eating as a sacred act of community trust in God. Or who fast from consuming as an act of receiving life from God.

Instead of sloth, imagine a people who are zealous to do good works and who refuse sloppy thinking because it is an affront to the One who created them.

Instead of pride, imagine a people who humbly lay down their lives in service to others. Imagine a people who live selflessly with God at the center of their attention and put others in peripheral view.

Instead of lust, imagine a people who abstain from sexual intercourse until they are married, because they view the act as a sacred bonding of flesh to flesh, life to life.

Instead of greed, imagine a people who sit prayerfully with their checkbooks asking divine guidance on where the money should go. Imagine a people who stop working and accumulating once every seven days simply because their God told them to rest on Sabbath.

This is an odd people with odd practices in a world very unlike them. Are you open to being this odd?

I'm not hoping for a return of prayer requests for soap opera characters, "chitlin" frys, or guest artists coming to church hoping to get on stage. But I would be happy to see people who Sabbath well, save sex for marriage, give generously, eat gratefully, serve diligently, and live unselfishly. They would definitely be odd. Odd like God. And I tend to believe that the world would notice the difference in us and take notice that we are the treasure of our God.

Do we wish to be made holy, to be made like Jesus by sanctifying work of the Spirit inside us?

My wife, Denise, has captured the heart of our 4-year-old granddaughter, Eleanor Grace. They are two peas in a pod. When Eleanor Grace had her first hair salon experience, she was asked how she'd like her hair cut. Just like Grandma's. Who does she want to sit by at the restaurant? Grandma. Last week they were talking about wounded animals. Eleanor Grace loves animals. Denise explained what veterinarians do and suggested she might grow up to be an animal doctor. She shook her head no. Well, what do you want to be? She didn't answer with words. Eleanor Grace simply looked into Denise's eyes and pointed at her.

When love so consuming captures our hearts and we think about who we wish to be, the best we can do is point toward God and say, "I want to be like you." Odd like God. Holy. Just like Jesus.